Copyright 2018 reVision

All rights reserved. Printed in the United States of America. No part of this publication may be reproduced, stored in a retrieval system or transmitted in any form or by any means, electronic, mechanical, photocopying, recording or otherwise without the written permission of the publisher.

To the gals trying to launch a dream while also sitting in the carpool lane... you're the real success stories.

Introduction

When it comes to business, no matter what level you may be operating on, there's a real need to understand and control your money. Businesses are not successful without also being intentional in all that is done... especially when it comes to money, budgeting and financial aspects of business. However, so many women I've encountered are in denial when it comes to the numbers that make up their business. Fear and overwhelm can drive women away from this topic. It becomes easier to avoid the numbers than it is to dig in and do the hard, but necessary work.

Let me offer this disclosure.... I am not an accountant nor a financial expert. I am, however, a business woman who's learned all the wrong ways to handle money. It's my hope that through this book, my experiences will help you avoid some of the pitfalls I experienced and had to bounce back from.

This book is meant to help you start taking needed steps to put the dollars and cents in place. There're some aspects of this book that are technical, but even so it is basic. Other aspects are more focused on mindsets and methods surrounding money for your business. In the end, nothing can compare to the advice and counsel a great accountant can offer you and your business. When it comes to taxes and all that is due to the IRS, lean on the experts. Your job is to make money a priority and to NOT spend every dollar that comes into your account.

That being said, let's dive in and get real cozy with the calculations for success. I bet in the end you'll have a whole new outlook on money and maybe, just maybe you'll even like the money discussion!

1
Money & Your Mind

So much of what money means to our businesses starts with how we think and feel about money. Our personal experiences can shade our mindset toward financial matters even outside of the buck we make in our business. Before we can begin dialing in the processes that will help us better manage money, we need to stop and think about the mindsets we've already developed.

When there's a bad connection between how you feel and think about money, your profits will feel the impact. Clients and customers can catch a bad vibe when there's crisis surrounding your finances or when your desperate for a sale. You can easily tie motivation to grow your business with the money you make or aren't making. Money and mindset go hand in hand so it vital that we have it right.

Your mindset meter reading

Let's see where you stand on the money mindset meter. Answer these questions as honestly as you can. Most of the diagnosis for your money mindset lies in your heart. It's easy to say and do all the right things. But deep inside, you know how you truly feel and think. So, don't give me the "right" answers… give me your honest answers:

- T or F   I feel guilty charging full price for my products or services.
- T or F   I prefer to offer deep discounts for my friends and family.
- T or F   I get nervous when I have to tell a customer or client what they owe.
- T or F   My family/spouse/significant other takes my business seriously.
- T or F   I gauge what money I have to spend based on what's available in my checking account.
- T or F   I have a separate checking account for my business.
- T or F   I have a plan for saving money to buy larger items for my business.
- T or F   I am on track with the amount of money I have held back for taxes this year.
- T or F   I have a working budget for my business that includes day-to-day operating costs.
- T or F   I feel my pricing is spot on for my products and services.
- T or F   I know the value of my service, time and customer attention.
- T or F   My customers and clients are happy with the prices I charge.

- T or F I feel my pricing is competitive with my market and location.
- T or F I don't remember the last time I paid myself from my business account.
- T or F I have a written goal of what I want to be making in the next three years with my business.
- T or F I believe to make more money, I need to work harder to create more stuff to sell.
- T or F I can get ahead in my business if I use credit or loans to boost my ability to make more stuff… knowing I can sell more, make more money, and pay off that debt.
- T or F I know the difference between revenue, profit and pay.
- T or F I know the exact costs to recreate, replenish or repurchase my products and services.
- T or F To gain more customers, I need to offer the lowest prices.
- T or F I offer a lot of great sales and discounts to get money in the door.
- T or F I have a plan and system to show appreciation to my best customers.
- T or F My prices are set around a formula, not a shot in the dark or good guess.
- T or F I have a system to keep my records organized and easy to find.

Total True: _____   Total False: _____

If your "true" answers outweighed your "false" answers, you are on the right track for your money mindset. If you have more false answers than true, don't worry! This is the perfect place for you to course correct that logic and get your mind focused on the right things to help you succeed. Each of these true and false statements will be addressed in this book, so take heart! The truth is, no matter where you landed, we all have room to improve our mindset when it comes to money.

Hobby or business

"How do I know when my business is a real business?" I have had this question asked in several coaching conversations. It's easy to get hung up on a business being a "real business" based on where it's located or if you have a website or even how many followers you have on social media. The fact of the matter is a business becomes a business when it makes money. Christy Wright, business coach and personality of Business Boutique has been known to define it this way:

"A hobby costs you money.
A business makes you money."

It may feel like your home-based business isn't a full-fledged entity because you don't sit on Main Street with a beautiful store front. But if you're making money, yes, even your business set up in the basement is a real business! Some women get caught up in the thought that their business will be a "real business" when it replaces their fulltime income. But again, if the business makes money, it's a business!

There was a time when state offices would issue engraved certificates when a business filed as a legal entity. Now, given the convenience of online filings, those have gone to the wayside. See... even state offices recognize that a fancy certificate, or even the fact that you've legally set up a business, don't define you as a "business."

There's a variety of steps you can take to set up your business. Thing such as setting up a bank account, designing a logo, buying a domain name, hiring an accountant, or filing your Articles of Organization are all steps you can take for your business. But don't let these steps trick you in thinking you have a business. Some businesses are making money without these aspects in place. It's not the steps you take, but the money you make that defines your business.

In my twenties, I launched a photography business. This was before digital cameras, so that tells you how old I am and how long ago this was! At the time, editing software and technology was slim, and photos required the photographer to get it right in the moment the shot was captured. Given my background in photo journalism, I had a passion for photography, but I was a little uncertain with my skill in portraits. So, I started getting my feet wet with some free portrait sittings. I asked a variety of people to sit for portraits to help me out. I did this with a variety of ages and in a variety of locations. In return for their help, if the photos were good, the volunteer could choose to order prints at my cost.

Although I had picked a name for my business and even designed a logo and had some business cards, my business was not making money. In those early stages of the game, it was costing me money as I gained some experience and built my portfolio. I had a photography hobby. But after a few months, I was able to start charging for my services and move from hobby to business.

How do you know if your business is making money? We'll get into the calculations for this question in coming chapters. In the meantime, if you're able to cover the costs for your business from its sales, you are on the right track. Sure, you might not be making what you want, but that's OK. We'll get you there! However, if you need to invest personal funds to keep your endeavor afloat, you may be looking at a hobby. There's nothing wrong with that status. You can keep reading this book and working toward your goal of owning a business. We all started in "hobby" mode and with some concentrated effort and planning, you can transition into money-making mode.

Let's reFocus:

Go back and review your answers to the true / false exercise. What are some mindsets you can improve on? Jot them down here:

Are you in business mode or hobby mode? What does it look like to be in business mode versus hobby mode?

2
Money Mantras

I truly believe that women and men approach business differently. Where men may be more apt to look at the dollars and cents in black and white, women tend to be more intuitive. That's certainly not a bad thing, however, because we are more likely to lead with our hearts and let our souls map our direction, there are some beliefs that tend to creep into our minds that if left there, can derail our success. So let's take some time to identify some positive money mantras to overwrite the negative thoughts that may already have taken root our minds.

Making money is a good thing

Somewhere over time, be it due to pushy sales people or cheap tricks, we've developed a negative attitude toward making money. Women, more than men, tend to struggle with money-making guilt. There's a negative belief that we shouldn't charge for our products or services and that we should practically give away that which we are talented enough to create and produce. This is a limiting believe and not true at all!

Making money is a good thing! When you make money doing what you are good at and what you love, you can provide for your family, your goals, and your financial future. Making money means you can grow your business to the point where you can offer job opportunities to others. You might be able to lease a store front, adding to your small town's growth and redevelopment. Maybe making money means a way for your kids to experience dance lessons, play sports or even go to college. This grows their confidence, abilities and provides for their future.

"But I want to help people." This is a common justification for business women who routinely offer their products for free or deeply discount their services. While the heart behind this concept is rooted in good intentions, you'll only be able to help others for so long before you're bankrupt. Take a look at some of the most charitable corporations today. They are able to give and give greatly because the company has great resources to give out of. Why is that? Because they have charged a fair price consistently in order to make a profit. Those profits managed appropriately has led to an abundance from which they can give back.

"My friends and family don't want to pay full price." So many businesses start because friends and family fall in love with something you make or offer. It's easy to start selling to those that eagerly support you and want you to succeed. However, at some point your business must be treated as such and free or nearly free products are not viable. You need to charge a fair price to all your clients and customers. And, while it may have been easy to start selling to friends and family, it is imperative that you branch out to non-friends and non-family members in your customer base. You can't build financial success on friends and family alone.

Run on a planned path

Create a vision for your financial success that is built so that your business can run on a planned path. Too often when sales dip or customers grow silent, business owners are tempted to jump ship or run after something new. I have seen it over and over again. A business seems to slow down or even stand still and the solution becomes to throw a new product or service into the mix or complete jump ship and launch a completely new business.

I can't even begin to express the whiplash this causes your customers and clients. In business, there is times of feast and time of famine. There are seasons where things are booming and seasons where things are quiet. You'll experience plateaus, valleys and mountain tops. But this should not change the direction of your business.

A well-planned business knows the path its

traveling. It stays the course to weather the storm. And while it is important to keep evolving to stay with the demands of your market, there is a difference between evolution and disruption.

I worked with a woman who operated a direct sale business with some success. She had climbed a few rungs in the company's structure and came to me to help her to the next level. When things seemed to come to a standstill, she completely uprooted her business and in a week's time she had started a completely new direct sale business. It wasn't a few months later that she was doing the same thing.

Clients and customers can only make the jump so far and so many times. They depend on knowing and trusting your product and service line. When you take a sharp right just because you experienced a bad month, you stand to lose the loyalty of your customers. Keep to your vision and hold true to your plan. Don't jump the tracks just because you're traveling through a dark tunnel. Chances are you will come out the other side.

Be sure you've developed a viable vision for your business and ensure you have a clear plan for your finances that take into account the ups and downs of sales. Work smart not hard

More work does not equate to more money

I can remember holding commission positions that were sales related in my early careers. While these positions allowed for a lot of freedom, there was a false sense of security that when I needed more money, I just needed to work harder. But this is a misnomer. In sales positions as well as in entrepreneurship, simply turning up the number of hours you work doesn't mean you turn up the dollars you make.

The other trap that can grab us is the belief that when a financial crisis hits, we can apply more effort to get more money. Yes, there is something to be said for buckling down and pushing for a goal or stretching to reach a higher mark. But be careful that you don't abandon good financial sense for the belief more work equates to more money. The reality is a lot of hard work goes into growing a business, but it may take months for the financial rewards to come around. Consistent financial practices are always safer bet than relying on grit and grind to bridge financial lulls.

Choose to work smart, not hard and keep yourself to a budget that takes into account a stable savings plan and a clear evaluation of your actual profit. More on this topic in upcoming chapters.

Planned portions are better than leftovers

We know that when we make a sale, one hundred percent of the money we make goes into our personal pockets. We have to account for the cost of doing business, taxes and so on. However, older accounting methods would have you believe once you pay for everything, what's left over is your paycheck. While that theory is true, the mindset is dismal. You're left feeling like you've been paid in table scraps rather than a real wage for the talent, skill or product your offer.

A more flattering concept is the idea of planned portions for your personal pocket. If you designate a specific percentage for all your bases, each one is treated equally and there are no "leftovers" but rather a planned portion for each bucket that needs funded. Those buckets can include your costs, your taxes, your savings and your paycheck. No one bucket is more important or takes priority over the other. But a percentage of each dollar is designated for each bucket.

We'll unpack this concept later in this book, but for now I want you to start thinking differently. I want you to stop thinking as if every dollar is yours for the taking. On the flip side, I want you to stop feeling as if you can't pay yourself at all. There is a happy compromise and that lies in a planned percentage that proportionally divides each dollar, so every aspect of your business gets a little...even you!

Feelings don't balance your budget

Have you ever walked away from a really great sale and felt untouchable? I remember when I started my digital marketing company and landed my first contract to market for a local organization. I felt like a million bucks and that success boosted my confidence. I also remember feeling disappointed when I didn't get awarded a contract for a chance I was clearly best suited for. In both scenarios, my feelings were on the extreme, but I didn't allow that to impact my budget.

When we've made a great sale it's easy to feel like you have all the money in the world to do whatever you want. At the same time, when you've had a low month, you can feel fearful that your finances won't sustain your business. Scarcity can breed fear just like abundance can boost pride. Neither situation is good nor true since our sales can swing from one extreme to the next. And, remember, sales are not controlled by you. You can't make your clients and customers buy from you. Sure, you can put in place the best website and offer the best service and even have the best prices, but customers are still free to choose what to buy and who to buy from. That being said, a balanced budget based on thought-out numbers is far more stable and consistent that how you feel about your business. Don't let the emotions of the day's sales dictate your feelings of financial success.

Debt free is the best way to be

One of my dear coaching clients wanted desperately to take her business to the next level which for her meant increasing the number of products she provided and improving their quality. To do so, she needed more supplies and more equipment, which meant she needed more money. She opted to take out a business loan that offered her the money she needed to buy materials and machines to crank up the production. Although the terms of her loan were decent, she soon felt the pressure of making her dream really perform in order to make the payments and meet the demands. It quickly meant that every dollar went to the loan and although orders had increased, she felt a slave to her business and her business loan. It didn't take but about a year for her to burn out, resent her business, and regret her loan decision.

I am not a fan of debt. Having worked very hard to become debt free, I am would rather do anything else but take on a loan or rack up a credit card to make it in the business world (that goes the same for my personal finances… we don't do debt in our household).

When I first launched reVision, it was a simple online publication that only required the purchase of my domain name and the monthly subscription cost for my website. Total it cost $56 to launch. However, at the time that seemed like a fortune. I was recently divorced, living paycheck to paycheck working for a small newspaper in my area. The cost to start reVision needed to be saved and although I wanted to launch it the moment the idea came into view, I had to wait several months before I knew I not only had the $56 dollars to start but could cover the on-going the monthly subscription fee.

Could I have found some plastic to charge those first few months? Sure. Did waiting to save up the cash mean I started out of the gate a little slower? Yes. But I started without the weight of debt and without the pressure of my business needing to succeed. At the time, I had no idea if reVision would make it. And no new business owner can be more certain. Being in business is a gamble. You only increase the stakes when you factor in debt.

If you choose to close your business or put it on the shelf, your business debt does not go away and it doesn't wait until you make the money to pay it back. Regardless of the success or failure of your business, that debt is required to be repaid. It is much better to move slower and steadier than to race out ahead, straight into a wall of financial crises, debt and disappointment. Don't dismiss small beginnings. They are the ones that usually stand the test of time.

Let's reFocus:

Take a moment to answer the following questions and journal some thoughts about these money mindsets:

1) Making money isn't bad. Making money allows me to help others and grow my ability to give back.

2) My plan for my business is clearly set and even though I may have some bad days or even a series of bad days, I am going to stick to the plan.

3) I am going to depend on a good budget and not get stuck in the trap that I can work harder to make more money. I realize that while hard work is needed, the financial reward may not come for a while.

4) I will operate with planned portions spread across a few designated buckets and not get stuck simply paying myself whatever is left over.

5) My emotions about my success won't be dictated by the amount of money I am making. I am going to stay focused on what I love doing and understand that my passion and my paycheck aren't always equal.

3
Money & Marriage

It's been well documented that the number one reason for divorce in marriages today are money fights and money problems. The same pressure that can put the strain on marriages in personal finances exist in your business finances. It is hard to walk confidently ahead and be motivated to put the work into your business when your spouse isn't on board or your family seems to work against you. Whether your dating, married, engaged, have kids or not... this chapter is for you! Keep reading!

I learned early on in our marriage that I am the dreamer and my husband Mat is a bit of a realist mixed with nay-sayer. I will run to him with my latest and greatest idea only to have the wind knocked out of my sails by his realistic approach to make it happen. He isn't intending to be a bully, it's just the way his brain works. He's just the sort of personality I need to help balance out my entrepreneurial spirit that literally has a new idea every few hours.

We've learned to have communication style that is healthy for us both. It let's me get excited over a new idea and at the same time allows for Mat to vocalize his concerns on what it might take to launch the plan. The trick is to give me 48 hours. I come to Mat with an idea and of course to me it's the best idea since sliced bread! Although Mat's instincts are to ask a million questions, his role in the moment is to simply nod his head and let me be excited. If in 48 hours I am still excited and hooked on this idea, then we will sit down and make a plan to address both of our points of view. However, more times than not, in 48 hours I have moved on to three or four more ideas.

The same goes for money conversations. You most likely have a different way to communicate amount money than your spouse. Regardless of who takes the reigns in this conversation, it is important that you get on the same page and work together… even in your business finances!

Women who dream - husbands who don't get it

You may have started this chapter and thought, "It doesn't matter what I say or do, my husband doesn't get it." But take heart, girl! He can get it… you just need to know how to help him see it.

Whether it's trying to get your kids to cooperate or trying to get your husband to take your business seriously, so much of it comes down to how you communicate and what's in it for them.

My husband loves to see me excited and happy. That high energy persona is what attracted him to me in the first place. But when all of that "energy" comes at him with a business plan or idea, it's hard for him to swallow. I know I can't communicate in just wishful thinking type statements. He won't get on board as quickly if I just paint him a picture of pie in the sky hopes and aspirations. What he needs is for me to think through some hard details such as:

- How much is this idea going to cost
- Where is the money coming from
- How long will it take me to recoup it
- What's it going to require from him
- How much time is this going to add to my already busy calendar
- What does this look like in real life
- What does this mean to our future and our family's goals

All these questions are ones I need to know how to address in order for him to feel comfortable and be on board with this idea. I might not have hard facts and figures, but he needs to know that I've given it some thought.

That's our communication style…what's yours? If you tend to be the big idea person, maybe he's the detail person who needs a plan and all the data. Maybe you're the one who likes to see the map before striking out on an adventure. Whatever it may be, the key to making money work in your marriage is to be sure that you are taking the other person's feelings and needs into account.

The same goes for the kiddos and the family as a whole. If you're working for a big goal and together you all need to sacrifice and work together to get there, there has to be something in it for each person. I'm not talking about bribes or manipulation. But I am talking about understanding what makes each person in your family tick. Not everyone in your family is going to be motivated by the sheer notion of your business dreams being actualized. But they may be motivated that the extra money puts them in dance shoes or let's them go to camp or take a vacation.

When it comes to business, it may be yours and you may be the one that everyone sees as the owner of that business, but it's really a family affair. Your marriage will be better off if you include yours spouse in the discussions and let him be part of what your trying to grow. You might be surprised at the insight and perspective he can lend. I know Mat's surprised me a few times!

There's more to this money discussion outside of

just your business. There's also the whole money chit chat when it comes to your personal finances. And believe me... your business money and your personal money have an impact on each other.

As I meet and talk to couples, especially women, I find there are a few common responses to marriage and money:

1) "I take care of it all - my husband lets me handle it"

2) "I let my husband handle it - I trust him to do it all"
3) "I have my money and he has his - separate money is best."
4) "We don't talk about it....ever."

There's just something about those Benjamins that create tension in a marriage. No matter how much you have, money is a touchy subject ... or it can be. I am here to tell you it doesn't have to be. But first, let me briefly touch on why the above four responses can be a recipe for trouble for your marriage.

"My husband lets me handle it all"

Marriage is a partnership. It's equal and it's shared. While your hubby may not be gifted with a checkbook, it is still important for him to be involved in the finances.

Often times, husbands duck out on the financial chore because the wife has allowed him to do so. It's not fun, it's stressful and he'd rather dodge the burden or hide from reality. And... if you are doing it for him, why should he be tied to the table each month to create a budget or balance the account?

However, I have seen firsthand how this situation ends... he'll spend money, you'll get frustrated because you had a plan. You make your feelings known, he may throw back how hard he works and how much money he makes. He feels parented as if he needs to ask your permission before making a buy. You feel like a bully because you are controlling the dollars. Eventually, this can lead to his resenting you for being controlling. Because he bucks your system, you hold tighter, unable to trust that he will appreciate your efforts. In this scenario, fighting ensues.

"I trust him to do it all"

The same thing goes here as it did in our last scenario -- partnership is non-existence and it can easily leave someone feeling left out. But in this situation, there is another issue to address. If the woman is totally relying on the man to make the financial decisions and plan for their financial future, what happens if the husband is no longer able to keep up with this responsibility.

Statistically, men pass away before women and if that holds true for the couple in this scenario, a wife may feel overwhelmed to have to suddenly handle the purse strings. She may not even know where all the money, savings and retirement accounts are! I have seen this time and time again. It leaves the woman vulnerable for financial scams and fraud.

But... you might be thinking, "We're young. I don't have to worry about this right now." Well, accidents happen every day and we are never promised tomorrow. Beyond that, what if your husband is out of town for work or on a trip? What if he is sick or laid up from an injury. You can't afford to be out of the loop by letting your hubby hold the basket with all your eggs in it! In this scenario, fear ensues.

"I have my money and he has his"

Again, I come back to partnership. While I do think it is helpful to sometimes set aside separate spending money, individual accounts that are not joint with your spouse can lead to trust issues. While it may seem like a simple solution to keep money and bills organized, it actually drives a bigger wedge between couples and gives the couple more reason to NOT talk about money. I find that in these scenarios, intimacy is halted and the potential to dream together and plan a future together gets choked out. Walls get built and it is easy to declare "this is mine" instead of "this is ours." In this scenario, entitlement and ownership ensue.

"We don't talk about it....ever."

This statement is rooted in avoidance. It's the idea that if we don't acknowledge it, we don't have to fight about it. But at the same time, if you don't acknowledge it, bills can be missed, savings depleted and there is no intentional direction for your finances. While it may be more fun to be care-free with the finances, when it comes to major issues, expenses or emergencies, you may find that your only outlet is to turn to loans, credit cards, and other financing methods. This leads to a cycle of spend, spend, spend, debt, debt, debt. In this scenario, every financial crisis is a major one and panic ensues.

So, what's the alternative? Lots of discussions.

Mat and I are far from perfect. We don't always make the right decisions with our money, but 99 percent of the time we are intentional. We have set goals as a couple and as a family for our finances and we all work together to achieve them. This didn't happen overnight. We've had to learn how to get good at this money and marriage thing. Here's a few of the lessons we've learned:

- I've had to learn how to get interested in something I'd rather not deal with. Mat's had to learn how to dial back the numbers to speak in a language I can follow.
- We've learned that having a detailed dollar and cents conversation by phone is not good for us-- I tend to get lost when I can't see it on paper.
- We've learned that having this discussion late at night isn't good because we are tired and cranky and our minds are shot at the end of the day.
- Through trial and error, we've learned that what works best for us is to have a budget/money meeting each week. We evaluate the current week's bills and spending as well as look ahead at the coming weeks.
- We tend to work best when our budget meetings at the same time each week. Most of the time this is early on a Saturday morning when the house is quiet, and the weekend hasn't yet started. However, sometimes life gets in the way and we must adjust our time to be on a Sunday afternoon or Friday

night. The biggest thing is that these meetings get done...period. Even if it isn't ideal.
- We've come to realize that while we both look at money differently, we each have something to bring to the table. Mat is the numbers guy who can figure our paychecks to the penny, while I am super organized and at our budget meetings, I keep track of the plan we put in place, what bills we've paid, when and how much we've paid and I keep the calendar so we don't lose track of important dates, holidays, and weird pay periods.
- Now after a few years of doing this, we look forward to our budget meetings. We find that the conversation typically turns from just dollars and cents to wishes and dreams. It was at a budget meeting where I first learned that Mat wanted to visit each National park in the country, that we both agreed that tithing to our church was important, and at a budget meeting we planned and budgeted for birthdays, vacations, back to school costs and Christmas shopping.

All-in-all this approach to money had helped us be a team. We work together, and we are stronger for it.... Mat's got his strengths and his perspective. And while my skills and ideas are different, they are equally important. I've even learned a thing or two from Mat while working on our retirement plans together. Working together is the ONLY way we can pay off debt and work our way to becoming debt free and financially secure. That has brought so much peace in our lives and in our marriage.

Let's reFocus:

How would you define your communication style when it comes to ideas for your business? Are you a big picture person or a detailed, fact-driven type of gal?

Think about the members of your family. What is something or someway your business success can benefit them?

When was the last time you had a sit down budget and money discussion with your spouse or significant other? Do you feel you are on the same page with your goals?

Do you feel you have his support when it comes to your business? What might you be able to do to better that situation?

4
Making Dollars Make Sense

Take a moment and give yourself a pat on the back for making it this far in the book! I am proud of you! I know for some of you, this topic of money isn't your favorite.

Part of the reason money tends to be a sticky subject for us is either because we don't understand it or we are overwhelmed at the enormity of the topic. So, let's take a collective deep breath and dive into some real techniques for money management. Don't worry…we're gonna take it slow and we are going to make it simple!

Defining the three P's

In business there are three P's you need to know:

- Payment
- Profit
- Paycheck

Payment is when someone pays you for your products or services. This is also known as revenue in the accounting world. Profit is the amount of money you have once you've taken your costs out of the payment you received. This is hard costs to create or repurchase your product or service.

Payment – Costs = Profit

Paycheck is for the money you get to put in your pocket after you take all the deductions from your profit. Deductions can be for taxes, savings, etc.

Payment – costs = Profit – deductions = Paycheck!!

It is important to know that these three things are not the same. They serve a very important purpose in defining money for your business and can make the difference between staying afloat and bankruptcy!

Let's take a real-life example:

You make a $100 sale. It costs you $25 to replace the product you just sold:

Payment $100 – Costs $25 = $75 profit

Out of that $75 we are going to hold $25 for taxes and another $25 for savings because you printer is on the fritz and you're going to replace it soon.

$75 profit - $25 taxes - $25 savings = $25 paycheck

In this scenario, you sold $100 but you are only putting in your pocket $25. Your paycheck isn't $75 or $50…it's $25. This is difference between knowing you made a sale and knowing what your paycheck is.

Just imagine that you made the same $100 sale but put all $100 in your pocket. You can only get away with that for a short time before you've ran out of products to sell. But because you didn't make a plan for replacing that product, you no longer have the money to buy more.

Your only options are to:
1) Close your shop because you have no more inventory to sale,
2) Use credit to advance some cash or financing to replace your stock (and hope that you can sell it…. Not putting any money in your pocket because now your formula has to take into account a loan payment) or
3) Take all the money you would have paid yourself and slow reinvest it in your products.

I think we can agree that these three scenarios are crummy options. But those are the options you'd be faced with if you didn't know and follow the three P's.

The same scenario plays out if you don't hold money back for taxes. You'll either be staring down a big tax bill or having to close. If you get hit with expenses and haven't held any money back for them, again you are faced with closing or leveraging what you have to take care of the cost.

"Oh, I've got personal savings I can dip into." I've heard that a million times. Remember that chapter we just read on money and marriage? Nothing makes a spouse start to doubt your business success than you having to dip into the personal account to cover business expenses. When was the last time Target CEOs pulled out their wallets to make up the budget? Big corporations don't do it and you shouldn't either!

"Oh, I'll just run a big sale and ramp up my numbers to get me back on my feet." While we all love a good sale, this is not an answer. Not only would you not be taking a paycheck because your dollars would be reinvested in the business, but your percentages would be less if you drop your price. Meaning, you'd have to sell more to make the same amount of money as you would if you were selling it at full price. Plus, you run the risk of liquidating your stock at a rate faster than you can afford to replenish it.

"I don't have products. I have services, so I don't really have anything to replace." While you may not have a physical product to exchange for dollars, you do have operating costs. You better believe that your website company wants their money for hosting your site and the office supply company wants to be paid at the register when you need more paper to print out your lessons, recipes or instructions. Every business has a cost. You need to plan to cover those costs.

Bucket budgeting

I want to introduce you to a very basic budgeting principle that has held true for every business I've owned or worked in. It's called bucket budgeting. Now, there are accountants and professionals that would give you more scientific and expert advice… go see them and get that advice! I did.

In the meantime, however, I needed a simple way to keep my money straight. I knew if it wasn't simple I wouldn't do it. If I had to juggle a bunch of spreadsheets and complicated formulas, I would just fly by the seat of my pants and be bankrupt before the year was out. So… I started using this system, the bucket budget.

The bucket budget has four categories:
1) Replenish / reproduction costs
2) Taxes
3) Operating /Savings
4) Paycheck

Each bucket gets 25% of each dollar I take in. When someone buys a $10 book, $2.50 goes into each budget. Meaning, I get paid $2.50 while the remaining $7.50 gets split between replenishing that book on my inventory shelf, taxes for that item, and operating costs.

We've already talked about the importance of replenishing your inventory or products. That's the first thing that needs to come out of the payment someone has paid you. If you are service based business that is truly not offering a tangible item, then you may not have any replenishing costs.

Second, you will hold money back to taxes. You'll need to have a reserve for your tax bill come tax season. If it turns out you don't owe money for taxes, this is a bonus savings and you can choose to take it as a bonus or reinvest it in your business. Whether you have a product or service-based business, you will need to hold money for taxes.

Third, you will need to have some cash for operating costs. From website fees to pens and reams of paper, there is a cost for doing business that is outside of the actual cost to produce the item you sell. And if you are a service business, there is a cost to doing business for you too. Costs can include everything from membership fees to office supplies to your cellphone bill to marketing costs to travel expenses.

Finally, you get to the paycheck…your money! You may get through this calculation and realize 25% seems like you are working for pennies! That means a few things:
1) You might need to tweak your goal, realizing this might take a bit more effort or more time to cross the finish line.
2) You may need to increase or adjust your pricing.
3) You may need to see if what you're doing for a business model is scale-able, meaning can you do it on a large scale.
4) You might want to consider if you can create some evergreen, automated streams of revenue like an e-book or webinar that you don't have to recreate with each order…just let it live on your site and bring in the cash.

These buckets might burst your bubble a bit. Let's be

honest, $100 or $75 looks way better than $25. But the reality is, this calculation is important so that you have your financial buckets filled but also, so you know if what you're doing really is a business or a hobby. No one says the buckets must stay like they are... you can grow and evolve your business to where these buckets are overflowing. But you must know where you stand right now.

You might find that over time, your percentages can change a bit, but I've found them to be pretty darn close to perfect. And when it comes to saving for large purchases, I either take it out of my operating bucket if that will do or I take less of a paycheck to put some extra money in savings for the business.

Keep those buckets straight

To keep your buckets organized, I highly recommend a separate account for each bucket. I know that may mean some extra money moving but it's really not that bad once you get into the swing of it.

I have a checking account for my replenishing needs to restock my inventory, a savings account for my tax savings, and a checking account for my operating costs. I also keep a savings account in case I need to save for a big business expense. You can choose to do this with envelopes and deal with cash if you like. I did that until I had enough to put in each account to avoid fees.

Regardless, my business money NEVER mixes with my personal money and vice versa. So let me play out my scenario with the book purchase we used before.

- Someone buys a book for $10.
- I put that $10 in my business checking account.
- I transfer $2.50 into my checking account for replenishing my stock.
- I transfer $2.50 into my savings account for taxes.
- I leave $2.50 in my business checking account which I use for operating expenses, and
- I take out $2.50 for me as my paycheck.

Now, based on this equation, I may not reorder every book each time someone buys it. I might choose to make one big order once a month. If I've been putting that money aside all month long, when I got to make a big order, I have all that I need to do so. This replenishing costs should cover the cost of the book, tax and shipping costs for that order.

What if 25% doesn't cover your cost to replenish

your stock? What if it's 50%. That's simple! We just adjust the percentages:

Payment of $100
 – Cost to replenish of $50 = $50 gross profit

33% of $50 for taxes = $16.50
33% of $50 for operating costs = $16.50
33% of $50 for your paycheck = $16.50

All we did in this scenario is take what was left after replenishing the stock and divide it into thirds since the first category was already taken into account.

Let's look at one more scenario. What if your cost to replenish is $34 out of a $100 sale.

Payment of $100
– Cost to replenish of $34 = $66 gross profit

Divide $66 into thirds to fund your other three buckets:
1/3 of $66 for taxes = $22
1/3 of $66 for operating costs = $22
1/3 of $66 for your paycheck = $22

Let's reFocus:

Now it's your turn! Take an average sale and determine what your cost is to replenish those items in your stock. It may mean you need to take a moment to calculate what an item costs you to make or purchase wholesale.

If you buy six dozen roses for $1,440 you need to know what each individual rose costs you. If you buy bulk fabric, you need to know what each yard of fabric costs you and how much fabric goes into each dress or clothing item you make.

Take time to sit down and crunch these numbers. They don't have to be exact, but you do need to be realistic. Then take your hard costs to make that item and determine what percentage that is of what your sale price is. Are you satisfied with that percentage? Are you satisfied with what your paycheck really is? What adjustments do you need to make more to put more in your pocket?

This may take a little bit of time, but it is time well spent. The good news is it gets easier each time you do it and you can always make changes as you grow and get better. Visit christiebrowning.com to download a free budget guide.

5
Pricing Pitfalls

All the formulas and all the budget conversation can't make up for poor pricing. When you're starting out it is very challenging to know where to begin on price. I think this is hardest for service-based businesses because there's no hard costs to factor into the equation. We'll address this in just a second. But first, let's talk about those of you who sell a tangible product.

Product sales need to have two things considered when it comes to pricing. One, the actual costs to make or purchase the product. Two, the value of that item – meaning your expertise and talent factored in.

If you make handmade kids clothes, your hard costs include the fabric, thread and buttons needed to make that item. That's a no-brainer. But the other factor to consider is your quality, know-how and expertise you add into the item. Remember when mom used to say "it's made with love?" Well…there's a pricing factor to be considered for the cost of your "love."

To help you think along the lines of added value, consider if a seamstress came to you with years of sewing experience. She had worked for the top designers all over the world and now she wanted to work for you. You wouldn't just be paying her an hourly wage for sewing on some buttons, you'd value her experience and the know-how she gained by working with the elite. You have that same value. It's worth something and should be considered in pricing.

In this example, you wouldn't expect to pay the same price for these items of clothing as you would clothes at Walmart. There's nothing against the clothes at Walmart but that's a different product line that doesn't compare to a handmade item.

Speaking of expertise, this same factor should be considered for those who offer services. If you are a counselor or coach, there is a value to your expertise and know-how. I might be able to read a book and glean some helpful hints to better my relationships or gain better health, but when I work one-on-one or get more hands-on attention, I expect to pay for the service, the knowledge and the service of that expert. This is sometimes referred to as value-added billing or pricing. You are adding to the price because of the value you can add to that person's experience.

Photographers are popping up everywhere. Time spent with a camera you can buy on Amazon and a few editing software packages, you can call yourself a photographer too. But that doesn't take into account the know-how of manipulating lighting, posing and positioning as well as props and backdrops.

The pricing between photographers swing greatly from a few hundred dollars to thousands of dollars. What's the difference? The camera may be the same, the software may be the same...so what are you paying for? The skill of the photographer such as posing.

This is a great example of a service that has a special value attached to it. The tangible side in this example is the pricing for the prints. There are two marketable items here.

Let's talk about another example.... A trainer. Sure, you can go to the gym and run on the treadmill. But for an added fee you can pay for a personal trainer. There's nothing magical about the treadmill. What you're paying for is the trainer's expertise. There's value in that expertise and the personalized plan they can create for you.

Pricing pitfalls exist for all types of businesses in all types of industries. But take heart, you can dial in and tweak your pricing as you grow, evolve and learn more about what your clients want.

Pricing Pitfall #1: Being the cheapest

An easy temptation for any business is to look at the competition's pricing and simply offer your products or services for less. But beware. Being the cheapest is a race to the bottom where the winner loses their shirt and makes no money. Cheapest isn't always best and sometimes there is a perception with clients that you get what you pay for. So, if you are cheap, they might question your abilities or quality.

The other painful lesson on being the cheapest is that it isn't sustainable. You can't be the best in service and be the cheapest… at least not forever. Service and quality costs money and to deliver this consistently you need to charge appropriately.

Think about your favorite boutique. You love the beautiful store, helpful employees and the way the wrap your purchases in pretty tissue paper. Do they do that for you at the big box stores? No. Do the big box stores charge less? Yes. Do you continue to buy from the boutique? Yes, if you love the little touches that make that experience rich. Does everyone shop at the boutique or appreciate those service touches? No. And guess what… your favorite boutique is OK with that. They aren't trying to lure the big box crowd who is only concerned with price. They want the customer who appreciates the experience.

The lesson here is to avoid making "cheap" your goal. Look instead at who your ideal customer is and what they want. Do they want personalized service? Are they looking for customer service on a grand scale? Do they want to have special services available like alterations, gift wrapping, sizing, delivery, etc.

Pricing Pitfall #2: Always offering a sale

Gals, we all love a good sale. Who doesn't look for a full clearance rack when entering your favorite stores? But pay careful attention to those retailers and their sales. Typically, those sales come at the end of a season, as merchandise is being repackaged or phased out, when inventory is in abundance or when they need to liquidate some stock. They don't offer a sale for sales sake.

Like we discussed in our budgeting chapter, sales cut into your bottom line. You typically don't make as much money when you sell an item at a discounted price. Sure, it's helpful to make something rather than nothing, but you don't want this to be your go-to strategy for your business model.

Not only do sales lessen your profits, customers will get wise to the sales you hold if you hold too many. Why pay full price when I can just wait a week and get it on sale? If your customers see too many sales, they'll never pay full price. Be strategic in your sales and discounts. Be careful that you don't do them too often and too deep. Always remember what your costs are so you don't sell yourself short.

Pricing Pitfall #3: Pricing to the wrong people

We've already touched on this a bit but remember that your pricing is based on the people you truly are trying to sell to. Not all customers are yours. You are not trying to be all things to all people. It's OK that some buyers buy elsewhere.

There are a few points of sales to consider when you think about your market:
- Those who buy for high style
- Those who buy for high service
- Those who buy for high quality
- Those who buy for high savings

You cannot cater to all these buyers. At best you can cater to a few of these categories but not all of them. If you choose to produce a product with high style, you won't be the cheapest therefore those that buy for savings won't be looking to you. You may be high on quality and high on service, again, you won't be high on savings because those things come at a cost.

There is nothing wrong with being the business that

caterers to the buyers looking for savings. Companies like Walmart and Costco and others have built a fortune doing so. But do you walk into these establishments and expect to have a personalized shopping experience? No. They know what they are and what they aren't, and they don't try to blur those lines. You need to do the same.

Pricing Pitfall #4: Price guessing

If you are a new business who is green at establishing your pricing or if you are launching a new product or service and are having to determine your pricing, there is something better for you than just simply taking a good guess.

Consider these factors for formulating your price:
- Cost to create/buy/make your item
- Expenses to run your business
- Your time and value added to your item
- The quality that you provide
- What the market will pay
- What your location supports

We've already covered some of these factors. Now I want to spend some time discussing the market and your location.

What you can charge for an item in Indiana can be

ten times more in California. Don't believe me? Just take a look at the real estate in the Midwest versus the West Coast. There is something to be said for location. Consider where you're sitting and take note. Your pricing expectations need to consider where you are at geographically. If you sell online, you'll need a location average and quite possibly the location factor won't be as big of an impact on your pricing.

When we consider the market for pricing formulas, there is a major step you can take to help you dial in this facet of pricing: research.

Research your competitors. But be sure you are comparing apples to apples. Don't compare your boutique gift shop to Hallmark. Be clear on what the competition is doing as far as service, quality, and so forth.... Not just price. The goal here isn't to simply determine their prices and come in lower than them. No, the goal here is to let you get a feel for the market in your area. So when shopping competitors, be sure they are serving the same market as you are.

To be clear, the "market" is the customers that will buy or potentially buy from you. Markets can be made up of geographic location, age, gender, and background. If you're product caters to a 20 something crowd, don't shop a competitor that caters to a 60 something crowd. Get a look at like markets. Remember the goal isn't to beat them on price but to understand the market and what is already being offered to them.

The second research component is product testing. Whether it's a product or a service, find a handful of folks who are your ideal customers and offer them a trial. In return for their honest feedback, you can offer them the item for free or at a discount in the end. When I first started coaching, I offered to coach a few ladies I thought I would like to work with. They seemed to be the type of gals that resembled other women I'd like to have as clients. So I offered to coach them for free for a period of time. At the end of that time, I asked a few important questions and you should ask the same:

1) What did you like best about this product or service?
2) What would you change to make this product or service better?
3) What is this product or service worth to you?
4) How much would you be willing to pay for this product or service?
5) Who else do you know who would love this product or service?

Each of these questions can deliver very valuable

information which you can use to confidently market your item, price your item and introduce your item to other interested customers.

When you ask your test subject what this is worth to them, you are asking them to value the experience. The question of what they would pay gives you an idea of what they will spend to get that item. They will NOT be the same amounts. The experience should be worth more to them than what they will pay and that's OK. You want their experience to be priceless because they'll be loyal, grateful customers who appreciate what you offer.

Research is the best way to hone your pricing. The best part of pricing is that it can change. If you feel there is more room to bump that price up, go ahead! That's the beauty of being the boss.

But beware of price dropping just because there's a lull in your buying activity. Be sure you aren't in an off season, look to see if your marketing to the right people and in the right places, evaluate how you communicate about your product or service ... all of these things should be considered before lowering your price.

If you've done your research well, you should make lowering your price the last thing you do. Why? Because people hardly buy because of price. You need to know what they need and be able to communicate that you have the solution to their need. If you help enough people get what they want, you'll have no problem moving your products.

Let's reFocus:

How do you feel about your current pricing? Do you need to make some adjustments? Have you firmly calculated your costs for each product?

Who are some market competitors you could look to for some research on what your market will pay?

Who are some potential customers you can ask to product test for you in exchange for some good feedback?

6
Simple Bookkeeping Solutions

Now that you've done all the hard work of figuring out the dollars and cents of your business, it's time to make sure you organize yourself so that this information doesn't go to waste.

There are several software programs you can use to keep up with expenses and revenue for your business. These are affordable and offer good support should you need some help navigating the systems. However, if you aren't ready to go that route, and even if you do, I recommend a simple filing system to keep you covered.

You'll need 24 file folders, two for each month of the year. Label 12 folders as "Expenses" for each month of the year. Label the other 12 folders as "Revenue" for each month of the year. Example: January Expenses; January Revenue.

Throughout the month simply file each receipt in your expenses folder. When you make a sale, file your sales receipt or invoice in the revenue folder. You'll do this all month long being sure to include any expenses that might automatically be charged to your debit card.

At the end of the month, you'll need to group your expenses into like categories such as office supplies, marketing, fees and licenses, etc. You can track this on an Excel spreadsheet or simply on a piece of paper.

Write your categories and each corresponding expense on the sheet, totaling each category as you go. Finally, total your categories to get a final amount of expenses. Staple or attach your receipts to this worksheet.

Do the same thing for your revenue receipts and invoices. Once you've added it up staple or attach your receipts to this page.

On a third sheet of paper, transfer your total revenue amount and your expense amount. Subtract the two to get your profit or loss amount for that month. Also on this recap sheet, you can jot down your mileage for the month and any other write offs you know you'll need come tax time.

If you are diligent to do this each month you will have a concise way to offer your data to your tax preparer instead of dumping a shoebox of receipts on their desk. They'll thank you for it!

About Christie

Christie Browning is an encouraging author, empowering coach and inspiring speaker. Through live, inspirational events, group coaching for business owners, faith-based blogs and videos, as well as a variety of books, Christie reaches entrepreneurial & corporate audiences, faith-based groups and others. Her *#liverevised* movement has compelled followers to chase purpose-filled lives full of passion and possibilities while fighting to be free from past mistakes, failures and disappointments.

Follow Christie, sign up for her newsletter and get information on how you can book her to speak at your event at www.christiebrowning.com

www.ingramcontent.com/pod-product-compliance
Lightning Source LLC
Chambersburg PA
CBHW071433220526
45469CB00004B/1518